POPCORN

by Meryl-Lynn Pluck

Photographs by
Gwenda and Fiona Parker

RAINBOW READING

Popcorn.
It's good to eat.
It's fun and easy to make.
It doesn't cost much.
It's good for you.
And a few dried corn kernels make a big potful of popcorn in a short time.

- Take one big pot or pan with a lid.
- Melt 20 grams of butter.
- Add 2 tablespoons of popping corn.
- Put on the lid.

- Turn the heat to medium.
- Wait until you hear the corn popping.
- Shake the pot.
- Wait until you hear the corn popping again.
- Shake the pot again.

- When the popping stops,
  tip the popped corn on to a tray.

- Eat it as it is, or add a flavour.

Salt Flavour

- Melt 2 tablespoons of butter in the pan.
- Pour this over the warm popcorn.
- Stir it well.
- Sprinkle it with salt.

Sweet Flavour

- Heat 2 tablespoons of sugar in the pan with 1 tablespoon of butter.

- When it turns to a light brown colour, tip the popcorn back into the pan.
- Stir around.
- Let it cool before you eat it.